CAUGHT

BY
CHRISTOPHER CHEN

★

DRAMATISTS
PLAY SERVICE
INC.

NOTE ON BILLING

Anyone receiving permission to produce CAUGHT is required to give credit to the Author as sole and exclusive Author of the Play on the title page of all programs distributed in connection with performances of the Play and in all instances in which the title of the Play appears, including printed or digital materials for advertising, publicizing or otherwise exploiting the Play and/or a production thereof. Please see your production license for font size and typeface requirements.

Be advised that there may be additional credits required in all programs and promotional material. Such language will be listed under the "Additional Billing" section of production licenses. It is the licensee's responsibility to ensure any and all required billing is included in the requisite places, per the terms of the license.

SPECIAL NOTE ON SONGS/RECORDINGS

Dramatists Play Service neither holds the rights to nor grants permission to use any songs or recordings mentioned in the Play. Permission for performances of copyrighted songs, arrangements or recordings mentioned in this Play is not included in our license agreement. The permission of the copyright owner(s) must be obtained for any such use. For any songs and/or recordings mentioned in the Play, other songs, arrangements, or recordings may be substituted provided permission from the copyright owner(s) of such songs, arrangements or recordings is obtained; or songs, arrangements or recordings in the public domain may be substituted.

The world premiere of CAUGHT was presented at InterAct Theatre (Seth Rozin, Founding & Producing Artistic Director; Annelise Van Arsdale, Managing Director) in 2014. It was directed by Rick Shiomi, the sound designer was Elizabeth Atkinson, the costume designer was Rachel Coon, the set designer was Mellie Katakalos, the lighting designer was Peter Whinnery, the visual designer was Bill Ng, the dramaturg was Kittson O'Neill, and the assistant dramaturg was Erin Washburn. The cast was as follows:

LIN BO	Justin Jain
JOYCE	Jessica DalCanton
CURATOR	Christie Parker
BOB	Ames Adamson
WANG MIN	Bi Jean Ngo

The New York Premiere of CAUGHT was presented by the Play Company (Kate Loewald, Artistic Director; Robert Bradshaw, Managing Director) in 2016. It was directed by Lee Sunday Evans, the set designer was Arnulfo Maldonado, the costume designer was Junghyun Georgia Lee, the lighting designer was Barbara Samuels, the sound designer was Jeremy S. Bloom, the art installation concept was by Miao Jiaxin, the production stage manager was Megan Schwarz Dickert, and the production manager was Ian Paul Guzzone. The cast was as follows:

LIN BO	Louis Ozawa Changchien
JOYCE/CURATOR	Leslie Fray
BOB	Murphy Guyer
WANG MIN	Jennifer Lim

CAUGHT was developed, in part, at the 2014 Sundance Institute Theatre Lab at the Sundance Resort.

CHARACTERS

LIN BO. An artist. Chinese. Male.

JOYCE/CURATOR. A journalist./A curator.
Caucasian. Female.

BOB. An editor. Caucasian. Male.

WANG MIN. An artist. Chinese. Female.

SETTING

An art gallery with a podium and folding chairs set up for a talk. Throughout the gallery there should be distinctive installation pieces or a single piece inspired by the text of the play. Ideally the piece or pieces should have something to do with the intersection of China and the West, be subversive and sly in nature, and be visually bold.

NOTE

/ indicates overlapping lines.

CAUGHT

1.

The art installation is in full effect when audience enters the gallery. All house lights up for the duration of this scene. Audience should engage with the art as they would in a real gallery. It should not be clear when they are supposed to sit down in the chairs. When it feels appropriate, a member of the theater's staff should say a few words of introduction ("Thank you for being here," etc.) and conclude with: "...and now, I want to welcome the artist himself, Lin Bo." Applause. Lin Bo takes the podium. He has a typed speech he reads from throughout. It is strongly suggested that a slide show is employed throughout. He speaks with a Chinese accent.

LIN BO. Firstly I would like to thank [Insert any name that makes sense for the context of the show] from [Insert name of producing company], and the Xiong Gallery for hosting my work in this pop-up gallery here. After this profile of me in the *New Yorker* magazine, I have almost felt I am this...symbol of...all Chinese suffering. So I am grateful when I get to be an artist *(Indicates gallery around him.)*, which is what I am.

Usually my work is not displayed in art galleries. Usually it occurs directly in the real world. Here in [Insert name of producing city], and before this in Beijing. It is my work in Beijing that I will talk about tonight.

For those who have read this *New Yorker* article about me, some things I will say, you will know. But there is more. And I will have a memoir out next May for an even more complete story so anticipate that. Not that I am attempting to sell anything. But some of this I am taking from my book.

So I will begin. My name is Lin Bo, and I am an artist. And I know this sounds like an Alcohol Anonymous phrase, but in China it is not too different. Because in China it is not too easy to say you are an artist. Take myself as an example. I was imprisoned in a Chinese Detention Center for two years…because of a single work of art.

I will first try to say a few words about Chinese contemporary art. I say "try" because when I think about the China contemporary art scene, I cannot seem to see it clearly. What was contemporary for me three years ago will not be contemporary now, and in China, three years may render any community unrecognizable.

This…fluidness…will be familiar to anyone who knows modern China. In Beijing the most distinctive landscape feature is the construction site. Buildings are erected at the same rate they are demolished. A site of rubble represents something coming up or going down, or maybe both. It is the cycle of life and death compressed.

This pattern—of the city enfolding and eating itself—appears in the art world too. Take, for example, 798 Art District in Beijing—an art movement that transformed completely, from the inside out.

For those of you who do not know, 798 Art District is this miniature city within the city devoted solely to contemporary art. At first look it seems a miracle. In the heart of China's capital to see galleries upon galleries brimming with provocation: Distorted sculptures of Mao, murals mocking the Cultural Revolution. But take a closer look, and things are not as they first appear.

Is this *really* provocative art? The answer…is no. In truth, these provocations are smoke screens. In truth, it is *not* dangerous to poke fun at Mao in this manner anymore. It is in the official government-sanctioned history that "mistakes were made" in the Cultural Revolution. This is "subversion-lite" art. The *real* subversive artists, the original founders of 798, have long been evicted. In truth, 798 Art District is now a major, government-sanctioned tourist attraction.

In the end this is classic Mao. The appropriation of subversion to suffocate true subversion from within. Already there are plans for a Las Vegas makeover, with Cirque du Soleil style acrobatics. When this happens, the transformation will be complete.

I took in this fluidness around me and decided to create a *transient* art that reflected it. I painted calligraphy on buildings scheduled to be destroyed. I made sculptures from found objects in busy urban centers. If there was flux I wanted to move with it. If things were destroyed, I would be the one to set in motion their destruction. I did not document any of it. They were to disappear completely.

In time, I wanted to simplify even more. I began imagining art that not only existed to disappear, but art that never existed in the tangible world at all. I thought back to one of my influences: Lawrence Weiner, who wrote statements rather than made things. Instructions for art that could be made by others but was not required. The idea itself was the art. For example, one statement: A GLACIER VANDALIZED. Another: AN APPLE MOLESTED.

I know what you are thinking. But stop and think of the possibilities. If a work of art is initiated by a giver (the artist) but fully realized by the receiver (the audience), then what hypothetical art does is simply remove the middleman. The experience is condensed, pure intention and pure reception. The perfect vessel in which to send art through the tangled censorship forests of China.

Almost every act of modern suppression can be traced back to the June 4th Incident, the Tiananmen Massacre in 1989 in which hundreds of student protestors were killed. "No more protests," the government said, and tightened its grip like a vice. Textbooks and websites are now monitored, and activists cannot move an inch within their lives.

So what can an activist artist do? Well, Lawrence Weiner made "imaginary art." I decided to make an imaginary protest.

The primary symbol of my protest would be a logo. I would appropriate the Chinese signature chop, which would read, in big red calligraphy: "Rally. June 4th. 7 p.m. Commemorate the Dead." I would spread the logo through my networks: bloggers, graffiti artists. I would tell them to cover the city with the same image, the same call: "Rally. June 4th. 7 p.m. Commemorate the Dead."

Rumors of a mass protest would spread far and wide. Everyone would be waiting to go, unaware of one crucial problem: Inside the logo, no location would be mentioned.

And so. On June 4th, at 7 P.M., if all went according to plan, hundreds, thousands of people would be glued to their computers, to underground websites looking for evidence of a mass protest. And so at the same time, across China, across the world, people would be thinking about Tiananmen in unison. Guards might be dispatched to the Square, not knowing we protestors had already joined together, that the protest had already commenced.

The logo went viral. On June 1st, three days to the anniversary, it spread through the activist blogosphere like lightning. I began seeing it everywhere. Posters plastered on buildings. Stenciled on sidewalks. There were even rumors the government had taken notice. But I was not yet afraid; there was no real protest. There was nothing we could be caught for.

Then, on June 3rd, 10 P.M., a knock on my door. I looked through the peephole and saw a young, anxious man. "Help! I'm in danger!," he said. I opened the door a crack. I should not have done that.

I was taken to a "preliminary examination" room at the Beijing Bureau. A tired, middle-aged man sat before me. His name was Inspector Gao. He questioned me without emotion, like this was one of a hundred daily chores.

He seemed to have difficulty grasping this was art. *Was* it a real protest or not? A protest pretending to be art pretending to be a protest? How many people were involved?

Then, the danger zone. Gao started asking about my activist associations. And after a time he came to a person I did know: Yu Rong, a dissident artist. A legend. He had been arrested, harassed, beaten. So was Yu Rong the true target all along? I said I did not know him. Gao stared at me coldly then moved on.

At four in the morning, Gao suddenly yawned and stood up. He said: "We are drawing up a warrant for your arrest. You will be detained until further notice."

I lived in a cell with murderers, rapists, drug dealers, some on death row, some with five kilogram shackles on their ankles. Some wore handcuffs too, chained to these ankle cuffs, forcing them to stoop so their spines curled like shrimps.

Breakfast was watery milk powder with a rock-hard piece of corn bread. Lunch and dinner was oily cabbage soup topped with a single boiled vegetable. Sometimes I did not have bowel movements for a week. Sometimes we poured food down the toilet and heard rats in the piping, feasting. They lived off our discards and screamed if they didn't come, sometimes crawling through the toilet and we would chase them back inside.

We shared the cell with roaches, and other large bugs I could not name. They would fly in from above because half the roof was in open air. During storms we would get drenched.

There were beatings and interrogations. Every month. The same questions, the same circles. Names, names, names which I could not give because there had never been a plot. I was hit with a bamboo switch and sometimes an electrified club which would leave large scars that never healed.

One time after a questioning, my tormentor sat before me, smoking a cigarette serenely. And said to me then, in a calm, relaxed manner: "Of course we know you are innocent."

"Of course we know you are innocent," he said. "We know you are not connected to Yu Rong. But you see, I must do this. Even though we are all alone in our little hidden corner of the world. Why? Because of ritual. Because you had an idea of action, and so I must act accordingly. This is the ritual. The order of the country turns on it. Even if no one ever knows you are here, the ritual must be practiced. Because somewhere, somebody must be the keeper of truth. Truth that ideas are founded on something real."

This happened near the eight month mark. At this point still no warrant, no conviction. Still a hypothetical criminal. I have no way of knowing if these days of ritual will last forever. I will have sixteen more months to go.

And I will stop here. Thank you for your time.

Applause. He moves away from the podium.

2

Suddenly, unexpectedly, a highly theatrical environment. An office at the New Yorker. *Lin Bo enters. Joyce, a writer, and her editor Bob are already there. They stand when he enters.*

LIN BO. Hello Joyce, so good to see you.

JOYCE. It's good to see you too, Lin. And Lin, this is Bob, my editor, have you met Bob? Have / you two met?

LIN BO. I do not think so.

BOB. I feel like we've met.

LIN BO. Yes! Me too.

   Comfortable laughter.

JOYCE. So Bob just wanted to sit in if that's okay, he wanted to meet you.

BOB. I'm invisible.

LIN BO. I have been wanting to meet you / so…

BOB. Perfect!

JOYCE. Take a seat.

   As they are sitting down…

LIN BO. *(To Joyce.)* How is your ankle?

JOYCE. Oh you remembered! It's fine / now, thanks.

BOB. Oh your / ankle? What…

JOYCE. It was just a sprain, long / time ago.

BOB. Oh okay.

JOYCE. *(To Lin.)* But thanks! Thanks for remembering. Okay…so.

   They are settled in their seats.

First of all, how are things? How was… You had a talk at [Insert the name of the venue] right? How did that go?

LIN BO. Wonderful! Xiong Gallery and [name of venue] have been great supporters / of mine so…

JOYCE. Oh that's so great to hear.

LIN BO. It was a good talk. I told my story…

JOYCE. How is the work at Simon and Schuster going?

LIN BO. It is going very good.

JOYCE. That's what this talk was, right? For book publicity?

LIN BO. A bit, yes.

JOYCE. So you're having a good experience at Simon?

LIN BO. Yes, we are in…galley revisions right now. Is that right, galley / revisions?

JOYCE. Yeah that's / right.

BOB. Hey is Pam still there? At Simon?

LIN BO. I…believe so… I / am…

BOB. Okay sorry just a quick story. So you know how Pam is, right? So we had lunch like three years ago when I was at *Harper's* and she just kept trying to push this author on me, just wouldn't let go, you gotta do his short story, you gotta, you gotta! And she's holding her glass of water while she's just gesticulating like a madwoman and then she says: "This is the author of the future!" and she literally throws the water in my face…

> *Laughter…*

(Over laughter…) It's all over me! *(To Joyce.)* Do you remember me telling / you that?

JOYCE. Yeah I do.

LIN BO. So she is an extremely…forceful woman?

JOYCE. Wait, so *do* you know Pam? Pam Heller?

LIN BO. Now that you are describing her I think I might not. I think I / would have remembered her.

BOB. Oh you *don't* know Pam. Oh I'm sorry.

LIN BO. Oh no, it's okay!

BOB. Okay so who's your editor?

LIN BO. Mark. Mark Finn.

BOB. Oooo Mark. They put you with Mark?

> *He shares a slightly derisive laugh with Joyce.*

LIN BO. Is there something wrong with him?

BOB. No, no of course not! You're happy with him, that's what counts. But hey we should move on, I'm sorry for—I'm invisible, for real now.

Light laughter.

JOYCE. Okay, so um… Okay so the reason I wanted to talk with you… Thanks for coming by / the way.

LIN BO. Yes of course.

JOYCE. So as you know my *New Yorker* piece about you generated a lot of interest…

LIN BO. Which is great.

JOYCE. Yeah it is! As you know, since I forwarded you a lot of the emails we / got.

LIN BO. Yes.

JOYCE. And so we got this email from…from a professor, a professor of Chinese Studies at Stanford, Maurice Friedman, do you know him? Do you / know his work?

LIN BO. No, I do not think so.

JOYCE. He's pretty prominent in the field.

BOB. I'm sure you must have heard his name at / some point.

LIN BO. Yes, okay…probably.

JOYCE. So anyway we got this email from him and…

Beat.

So Maurice's particular area of expertise, as it turns out, is the prison system in Beijing, where you were held.

LIN BO. Oh wow no / kidding!

JOYCE. Yeah! And I mean of course he did extensive research, spent lots of time there, talked to a lot of ex-prisoners, and he even got to go *inside* and… / check things out…

LIN BO. Uh-huh… Wow that is great.

JOYCE. Yeah!

LIN BO. That he was able to gain access…

JOYCE. Yeah I know, I think he knows how to charm / let's put it that way.

LIN BO. Ah, okay.

JOYCE. So anyway, he was really interested in my piece on you. For obvious / reasons…

LIN BO. Of course…

JOYCE. And he had—He wrote me an email, with some thoughts about the piece…

LIN BO. I look forward to reading it!

JOYCE. So okay here's the thing. Just for right now I kind of want to keep the email close to the vest, because it's… It has some… I just… I don't want to alarm you.

LIN BO. O…kay.

JOYCE. I mean it's nothing bad, I just want / to…

LIN BO. I am sure I will be fine, / but—…

JOYCE. If we could just do it this way, again it's not a big deal, I just want to take this at my pace? Does that make sense?

LIN BO. Whatever works for you!

JOYCE. Oh great, that's great, and thanks for being so understanding.

LIN BO. Joyce, of *course* I will be understanding to you.

JOYCE. *(Genuine, heartfelt.)* Thank you. I knew you would be. Okay so…

>   *She briefly looks at laptop to regain her place.*

So I just want to start by…going over some reeeeally small details? Is that okay?

LIN BO. Yes of course.

JOYCE. Okay so… And bear with me here.

>   *Beat.*

What did you say you…ate again? In prison?

LIN BO. What did I *eat*?

JOYCE. Yes, and specifically…in the afternoon and night.

LIN BO. It was umm *(Trying to gather words.)* …why was something—was there a problem with / the food?

JOYCE. Oh no, no…

LIN BO. Did I eat something bad?

JOYCE. No it's nothing like that.

LIN BO. Oh okay, that is good.

JOYCE. So what was it again? What did you eat?

LIN BO. For…lunch and dinner?

JOYCE. Yeah, yes.

LIN BO. Umm… Well it was mainly…cabbage soup… That is what I told you, yes? For / your article?

JOYCE. Yeah it was. So it was *mainly* cabbage soup?

LIN BO. Yes.

JOYCE. So there might have been variations?

LIN BO. Umm…

BOB. Any potatoes?

LIN BO. Potatoes?

BOB. Yeah.

LIN BO. N-no not that I remember. Sometimes it was like a…like a mush, is that correct? Mush? So there…there might have been potatoes in there, I…why what is going on?

JOYCE. Alright I'm sorry, so…okay so… Professor Friedman—he actually did an in-depth study of—you were in Detention Center 7 right?

LIN BO. Yes.

JOYCE. Yeah he actually did a study specifically on that prison, on Detention Center 7.

LIN BO. Oh okay wow, small world.

JOYCE. Yeah, you know he went there, talked to people inside about daily routines, about food, so… And so in his email he asked—he mentioned that in his research he found that the daily meal there, for Detention Center 7, was potatoes… And there was nothing about cabbage soup.

    Pause. Lin nods, thoughtfully.

LIN BO. And when did he conduct his study, / because…

JOYCE. *(To Bob.)* When did / he…

BOB. Three years ago? Three or four?

JOYCE. Three or four years ago.

LIN BO. Okay I was there two years ago, so maybe…

JOYCE. But I guess it's—would the diet really have changed though, in one year, I think is his point.

>*Beat.*

LIN BO. It must have, yes? I was / there! I know what I ate.

JOYCE. And this is—No of course! And I just want you to know that this is… We just want you to be able to clear up any misunderstandings. So this is just an opportunity.

LIN BO. I see. Well thank you for this…opportunity.

>*Beat.*

I mean you—*we* also must consider that what is presented to outsiders—if he was allowed inside a prison, what he saw would have been highly, uh…choreographed. Yes? / Do you understand?

JOYCE. No that's true, that's true.

BOB. Yeah but are potatoes much better than cabbage?

LIN BO. I feel I am perhaps…walking into a trap.

BOB. No, no, no trap. It's just that…Maurice is at Stanford, and we take all questions we get very seriously, but we're also serious about giving everyone the chance to defend themselves. So it's—Joyce is absolutely right that this is an opportunity. For you.

>*Pause.*

LIN BO. *(With exasperation.)* So what is the—question again?

JOYCE. So the question is… Why would you say you had cabbage soup if you…if you might not have.

>*Beat.*

LIN BO. I guess my whole thing is… I actually lived through it? So my experience might…trump? His…scholarship? That is just where I am coming from.

BOB. He's…at Stanford.

LIN BO. Could I see this email? Joyce?

BOB. He's…at Stanford.

>*Long, awkward pause.*

JOYCE. So…um…another thing is that… Professor Friedman also said that… In your piece you told us that the cell was open air. But he said Detention Center 7 didn't have any open air cells.

LIN BO. *(Shrugging his shoulders, in exasperation.)* I lived in an open air cell for / two years!

JOYCE. It's just that…two things, now, don't match what a highly respected researcher knows to be true.

LIN BO. Maybe he was not really in Detention Center 7.

JOYCE. He was in Detention Center 7.

LIN BO. He could be mistaken.

BOB. But he's / at—

LIN BO. Even if he is at Stanford.

> *Pause.*

JOYCE. He also said that…additionally…some of the language you used…specifically the…"curled up like a shrimp." That…sentence formation. In addition to the cabbage soup. It all…

> *Beat.*

It all sounded familiar to Professor Friedman, because cabbage soup was the staple of prisons in the late 1990s and the…the prison memoir of the dissident Jiang Qisheng—he said he had cabbage soup with drops of oil, and he said fellow prisoners looked like curled shrimps.

BOB. So that's cabbage *and* shrimp, so…

> *Pause.*

LIN BO. In my truest of hearts I conceived of shrimp language on my own. And it is conceivable that two different people could come up with that image. It is what a person shackled from the wrist to the ankles looks like.

JOYCE. Sure, of course.

LIN BO. Perhaps we prisoners are thinking about food more often / than people who have not lived in prison.

JOYCE. No, no of course. Sure.

BOB. But what about the open air cell?

LIN BO. I was in an open air cell.

16

BOB. But there is no open air cell in Detention Center 7.

LIN BO. Did Professor Friedman check all the cells??

JOYCE. I don't want you to get angry.

LIN BO. I am not / angry.

JOYCE. Okay.

LIN BO. I am just a little…flabbergasted. Is that the right word?

BOB. Weeee/eellllll…

JOYCE. I'm not sure about that.

BOB. Flummoxed?

JOYCE. Listen, Lin. I genuinely want to reconcile this. I want us to find a solution here. Can't you help me? Throw me a bone? I mean, just *hypothetically*, what could have happened?

> *Pause.*

LIN BO. Well, if we are speaking hypothetically…

> *Pause.*

JOYCE. Yes?

LIN BO. If I were to give this professor the benefit of the doubt— which you seem desperate to do.

JOYCE. Lin—

LIN BO. I could conceive of the possibility that I could have… confused the name of the detention center I was held in. Is that okay for a hypothetical?

BOB. You didn't know the name of the detention center you were in?

LIN BO. If the mistake is on my end, I gave you a possible explanation.

BOB. I don't understand. How could you not have known where you were for two years?

LIN BO. Inside the prison they do not advertise the name of it. I might have overheard Detention Center 7 and made an assumption.

BOB. So are you saying that's what happened?

LIN BO. What other explanation could there be?

BOB. You tell us.

LIN BO. Tell you what?

BOB. What other explanation could there be?

LIN BO. I just told you.

BOB. So is this the official stance now? You weren't in Detention Center 7?

Beat.

JOYCE. It's just that…if this…is indeed a mistake, then what else could you be mistaken about? Do you see what I mean? We have to be one hundred percent certain about what we can take to the bank, or the whole *thing* could be invalidated. Even the parts you *are* sure about.

Pause.

LIN BO. All I can say is that… There is no way to accurately describe what it is like to be imprisoned. There is no way to truly capture the confusion or the…way your mind fluctuates. The truth does not lie in the specific facts but in the sensations, the helplessness and constriction, the walls closing in and that is your entire world. And there is simply no way you will understand what it feels like to know this one life you have been given is disappearing before your eyes on some stranger's whim and you can never get this time back. So did I eat cabbage or potatoes? What was this tasteless, watery mush made from? What does it matter? What does it matter?? Do you see?

Beat.

I have read Jiang Qisheng's memoir. I can imagine a scenario—and I am not saying this happened—but I can imagine a scenario where my mind plays tricks on me and I have conflated certain specifics, certain word choices with my own experience in prison. But it is still truthful. If I recognize myself in his words, then it is truthful, and only I can be the arbiter of my own truth.

Pause.

BOB. Have you heard of *This American Life*?

LIN BO. I have. Why?

BOB. There was an episode called "Chinese Chess," about a man imprisoned for eight months. Have you heard it?

LIN BO. I do not think so.

JOYCE. The episode contained a description of an open air ceiling, and descriptions of screaming rats in the toilets.

BOB. So you haven't heard that episode.

LIN BO. Honestly, I cannot remember.

BOB. Can't remember?

LIN BO. No.

BOB. So it could be one of those things where someone else's details seeped into your mind and they felt truthful to you so you retold them as your own.

JOYCE. Bob.

LIN BO. Alright.

BOB. Alright what.

LIN BO. I think I did.

BOB. Did what.

LIN BO. Hear that episode. I just…forgot for a second.

BOB. Forgot for a second. Okay.

LIN BO. I remember it was an American who was imprisoned, a white American, and he said of course he had a terrible time during his stay but in the end he was able to meet a lot of cool people and that he did not regret it happened. A bit like my experience, right?

BOB. Oh god, please. Don't do that.

LIN BO. Do what?

BOB. Don't make this about race.

LIN BO. I am just relating / how I received—

BOB. No you're trying to deflect the narrative with white guilt.

LIN BO. I am not deflecting the narrative with white / guilt.

BOB. *(Sarcastically.)* Oh no! We'll never understand what it means to be Chinese because we're white. *(Out of sarcasm mode.)* Don't even go there. I am so over that.

> *Pause.*

JOYCE. Look, Lin. Even if your story is truthful by your standards… If it's not truthful within the standard parameters of truth, the *reasonable* parameters of truth, then it's problematic. Very problematic actually. For the *New Yorker*, for yourself, for your publisher, but especially, especially for me. Do you understand?

Long, very uncomfortable pause.

BOB. Well? Do you have anything to say?

LIN BO. *(Almost in a whisper.)* Can I…

BOB. What?! What?! Speak up I can't hear you! What?!

LIN BO. Can I!—… Can I speak to Joyce…on my own.

BOB. Anything you can say to her, you can say to me.

LIN BO. I feel comfortable with Joyce, and I want to talk to her.

BOB. No way. I'm not gonna let you talk to her alone, let you get her on your side. Nuh uh. Not happening.

Long, awkward pause.

LIN BO. Okay…okay…umm…yes…I made things up.

Pause. They are waiting for him to continue.

JOYCE. Made what up exactly.

LIN BO. The things you said. I embellished my prison experiences. They were not as…vivid as I described them. No fellow inmates shackled from head to foot. No rats. No rain coming through the ceiling. I did eat potatoes, you were right, but I thought cabbage soup sounded more dramatic so I substituted. And…I will also admit…I was not interrogated every month. It was twice. Maybe three times total.

JOYCE. Is that it? Is that all you lied about?

BOB. Of course it's not.

JOYCE. I want to believe it is.

BOB. Everyone knows a lie is like a cockroach. Seeing one means there's a hundred you're not seeing.

JOYCE. It's just hard to accept. So is there anything else, Lin? Why did you embellish your prison experiences?

LIN BO. Because…because…

Pause.

Oh fuck it I'll just say it. I was only held for three months.

JOYCE. Oh god.

She buries her face in her hands, almost crying.

LIN BO. Look, I'm sorry.

JOYCE. This is so bad. This is so, so, so, so bad.

LIN BO. I didn't mean to mislead you.

JOYCE. But you did. You did mean to mislead me.

LIN BO. I didn't mean for you to…find out…

JOYCE. Well of course you didn't.

LIN BO. Or be hurt by it.

JOYCE. Well I am. You hurt me. And you'll have to live with that for the rest of your life. God how could I have been so stupid. Do you realize this puts my entire career in jeopardy?! Why did you do it?

LIN BO. I don't know.

JOYCE. Just tell me so I can understand.

LIN BO. I wanted to share my experiences. I wanted to expose the government's treatment of me, but I felt I could only reach a wide audience if my experience was more sensational. But please believe me. My intention was good. Prison changed me profoundly and how else could I tell people?

Eerie soundscape.

BOB. Now how about…telling us the rest.

LIN BO. What do you mean?

JOYCE. Yeah what do you mean, Bob?

BOB. He's shown us five cockroaches, where are the other ninety-five?

LIN BO. I don't understand.

BOB. You were never in prison, were you.

JOYCE. What?!

BOB. Tell her.

JOYCE. What's going on?!

LIN BO. I don't know what he's talking about!

JOYCE. Bob, what are you talking about?!

Beat.

BOB. Am I right? Am I right, Lin? Did you make up the entire thing? The whole story? I can see that you did. I'll stake my career on it. I'll resign if you even set foot in a Chinese prison, that's how sure I am that you're a little lying piece of shit. Just say it. You're caught. It's over. Your accent doesn't seem right anymore. Own up and get it over with.

JOYCE. Is it true, Lin? Is it? Please say it's not true… Please just say he's wrong. Say you were in prison. I need you to be in prison.

Pause. She backs away, trembling in horror, crying.

Oh god… Oh god it's true… OH GOD IT'S TRUE! Oh my god oh my god oh my god…

Bob gets up and holds her.

BOB. There there, shhh… There there…

JOYCE. He made it up… He never went to prison…

LIN BO. Joyce…

JOYCE. You lied… *(Shrieking.)* YOU LIED!!… What else did you lie about? Was there even an imaginary protest?! Are you even a fucking artist?! Do you even know Yu Rong, the legendary artist Yu Rong?! Who the fuck are you!!!

A beat while she trembles and tries to control herself.

BOB. Bravo… Are you happy with yourself?… I just can't believe we fell for—or that *Joyce* fell for your shit… God… Does it feel good?… To take advantage of someone's trust?… A good person's trust?… In my book a person who betrays a good person's trust is the scum of the earth… Scum. Of. The. Earth… God I… I… I hate you… You disgust me… Just looking at you makes me want to… Want to… God I hate you… GOD I HATE YOU SO FUCKING MUCH!!!… GODDAMNIT!!!… You stink… Eww… You smell… Pfffughh!… Ughh… Take a shower!…

Pause.

(Roaring.) GODDAMNIT!!!!!

He goes on a rampage, destroying the office. Joyce does breathing exercises. Soundscape transitions into music underscore that is more gentle, more serene.

JOYCE. Lin, this story…was a big deal for me. It was my first big story for the *New Yorker*. It was my career break.

BOB. I don't know if we can let her write again.

JOYCE. I just don't think you know how hard it is to toil at the bottom of the journalism food chain, just working and working in the mines with no daylight in sight. So this was a big deal for me, a big, big deal in the microcosm of my life which I know from the outside seems like a privileged white girl's life compared to all the suffering in China but I am a living, breathing human too. So you might have blown a human life. Do you understand? I wanted to rise with you. The time we spent together was so meaningful to me. It felt like borders and cultures were just melting away. Did you feel a connection too? Or was that all part of the ruse?

> *Lin nods his head.*

LIN BO. I did, Joyce. That's one of the reasons the lie kept spinning out of control. Because I wanted to keep pushing this connection we had. The way you looked at me. The way you actively listened to me. The way your brow furrowed in compassion and sympathy. My love of those things…was real.

> *Music gets more beautiful. Lin's accent gradually disappears entirely.*

JOYCE. *(Through tears.)* You didn't answer my question from before. Was there an imaginary protest?

LIN BO. *(Through tears.)* Well sure. If it's imaginary then it happened just by thinking it.

JOYCE. *(Through tears.)* But did you even reach out to bloggers in Beijing?

LIN BO. *(Through tears.)* No… There was never an imaginary protest outside of my mind. I'm not even from China. I'm from Los Angeles.

JOYCE. *(Through tears.)* Wh—what?

LIN BO. *(Wiping away tears.)* I'm really straight-up American. I grew up near Venice Beach. I'm a performance artist. I just wanted to be part of the cultural elite so badly. So I figured the only way I could sneak my way into the club was to use my Chinese-ness to my advantage. So I came up with this story.

BOB. What is your real name?

LIN BO. I'm Fred Goldstein. I was adopted.

BOB. *(Gently.)* I understand. I get you. You want… You want to be white. Don't you.

LIN BO. *(Nods.)* Yes. Yes I do.

BOB. I am so glad you came clean. I feel like… now that you admitted this…we can finally move on. Do you feel it too?

LIN BO. *(Crying again.)* I do!

> *They all weep. They all do a group hug. Music swells. Lights out.*
>
> *Lights back up. Actors take a bow.*

3.

> *All house lights up as the cast is standing there. Curator comes forth in the midst of the applause. Two chairs are set up in front of the audience as she speaks and as actors disperse. The following introduction may be altered and tailored to match the specifics of the production. The following paragraph is a suggestion. Wang Min speaks with a Chinese accent.*

CURATOR. Thank you all so much for being here. My name is [Insert real name of actress]. I am an actress, as you just saw, *and* I am also a visual arts curator. So it was back in, I think it was [Insert a year that's about two years prior to production]? Is that right? *(Looking for someone offstage for a response.)* …When Xiong Gallery and [Insert name of producing company] started collaborating on Chinese artist Wang Min's newest work, which became the extraordinary hybrid theater/art installation piece you just experienced. I was so fortunate to have been brought into the process early, kind of as a…*bridge*…between the art and theater components. I ended up working very closely with Wang Min, and it's been such an amazing experience. We are so lucky to host her. She's here with us tonight, all the way from China. Please give her a round of applause.

(Over applause.) Wang, do you want to come up here?

> *She does, more applause.*

Wang has agreed to—you still okay with this?

WANG MIN. I am, yes.

CURATOR. Wang has agreed to talk with us a little about the piece. So Wang, do you want to start by talking a bit about the… germination of the piece? I know it was sparked by something very specific.

WANG MIN. The piece was first inspired by incidents of scandal involving truth and lying in the United States. Brian Williams, James Frey. But I was particularly interested in the Mike Daisey scandal that occurred here back in 2012. And for those of you— does everybody know about…

CURATOR. So Mike Daisey—if you want me to…

WANG MIN. Yes please.

CURATOR. Okay so just very quickly Mike Daisey was a—is a monologist, a theater monologist who performed a show called *The Agony and the Ecstasy of Steve Jobs*, about treacherous working conditions in the Chinese factories that make Apple products, and it turned out a lot of his…reporting…

WANG MIN. Or *content*…

CURATOR. Right, because I guess he was never a reporter, so some of the content in his monologue turned out to be…exaggerated.

WANG MIN. Or *dramatized*.

CURATOR. Okay, sure.

WANG MIN. His Apple factory research is true, the surrounding story of his journey in China has dramatic embellishments.

CURATOR. Ah, okay.

WANG MIN. And so he goes on this variety show *This American Life*, I am guessing many people…

CURATOR. Yeah I think most people know it. Though they might not call it a variety show.

WANG MIN. Okay, so Mike Daisey goes on this program to talk about the Chinese workers, and excerpts of his monologue are aired.

His story generated a lot of interest. Big success for everyone. But then the host, this Ira Glass, discovers key parts of the monologue are heavily dramatized, even fictionalized. This is a big problem, because his program had presented the whole story as fact. So Daisey is brought on the show a second time and is in essence…crucified on the air for lying…by Ira Glass.

CURATOR. And it was just this excruciating interview.

WANG MIN. Yes exactly.

CURATOR. So what caught your interest in this incident?

WANG MIN. One of my main points of interest has always been America's relationship to truth, particularly in relation to other countries.

CURATOR. *(Understanding.)* Mm.

WANG MIN. America places a high premium on "truth." No persons of any other culture get more defensive when questioned over their "truth." This piece of journalism must be absolutely, empirically *true.* This piece of art must be emotionally *truthful.* So when a glitch in "truth" occurs, the impulse is to defend and argue your own "rules of truth" to the death.

CURATOR. So it's—"truth in journalism trumps truth in art…"

WANG MIN. Exactly. And in the meanwhile, the real *content* of truth—workers' conditions in China—gets sidelined in the conversation. This is what captured my imagination—how arcane American truth battles reveal the hollowness of her global outreach.

CURATOR. Arcane American truth battles. I like that.

> *Wang Min smiles and nods.*

So this is a departure for you, isn't it. You're primarily a visual artist, and yet you chose to have a theatrical component to this piece. And on a personal note I just have to say how much fun it was to participate / in it.

WANG MIN. It was fun to watch as well.

CURATOR. Can you talk a little about that?

WANG MIN. About…how fun it was?

CURATOR. Ha, no sorry, about *why* the theater component to this piece.

WANG MIN. Ah I see. So Mike Daisey is a theater artist; and as per his perceived rules of his medium, he allows himself to stretch truth in order to craft a compelling narrative. But when placed in the context of NPR and *This American Life*, he runs into problems. Different medium, different rules. There has been a lot of this. Take James Frey for example, who is crucified by Oprah for his book *A Million Little Pieces*. Again, a confusion of category—if he had called it a *fictional* memoir, no problem. Non-fiction? Big problem. What interests me is this rift that occurs when different sets of rules bump against each other. We open a great chasm of unknowing. We see we do not know anything other than the architecture of our own rules. So it is this rift I seek by mixing theater with visual art.

CURATOR. I see.

WANG MIN. The dislocation is set in motion from before the beginning, with publicity. The piece was advertised in both visual art and theater circles, so this current audience is from two worlds, each with distinct sets of expectations. Both groups will be confounded by the blend that confronts them.

The confusion begins when you enter the space. Is this a gallery or a theater? When is the "show" going to start? Or has the "show" already begun? We move forward to the "show's" beginning. Again, a confounding of mediums. A man stands before us and speaks. It is a preemptive book tour, but with shades of a TED talk, and yet the whole thing is a "theater monologue," delivered by an actor, *and* we are in a pop-up art gallery.

We have four different mediums bouncing off each other. What do we hold on to? His story? And yet in the second temporal phase, his story is negated. More confusion. It is absolute chaos, orchestrated by an extraordinary group of theater artists—a playwright, director, actors, including yourself—who have been collaborating to create material based on my prompts, yet at our core, we are working in tandem to undermine each other.

And so we arrive now at the third temporal phase of the piece, where the artist is interviewed. Here, through our conversation, we hope to break any remaining authoritative bonds of appropriation, in order to move into a more foundational realm of truth.

Slight beat.

CURATOR. Can you explain that last part a little more? For me at least.

WANG MIN. Explain what?

CURATOR. Well let's start with "authoritative bonds of appropriation." Is that right?

Beat. Wang Min seems taken aback.

WANG MIN. Okay yes, yes.

CURATOR. Do you mean… Well I guess I really don't know what that means.

WANG MIN. And just so I am clear…everything else I said makes sense?

CURATOR. Y—… Yes. For the most part.

Pause.

WANG MIN. Okay…hm… Let us try this. At the heart of this Mike Daisey scandal is a…chain of appropriation. You would agree, yes?

CURATOR. Um. Sure, okay.

WANG MIN. Daisey appropriates a Chinese story, Ira Glass appropriates the same story filtered through Daisey. At each level of appropriation, a new set of rules, a new authority structure grafted on. Does this make sense?

CURATOR. Sure.

WANG MIN. Okay so *this* work seeks to *disrupt* this chain. Each segment presents the audience with a new set of rules, each embodied by a new authority figure. When these rules are deliberately questioned, so is the representative authority, and the chain of appropriation is broken.

CURATOR. Just out of curiosity, this term "chain of appropriation"…

WANG MIN. Yes…

CURATOR. Because the word "appropriation" has such negative connotations. So you think Mike Daisey was "appropriating" the stories of workers in Chinese factories?

WANG MIN. He appropriates them because he makes them his own.

CURATOR. Oh so it was because of the embellishments he made.

WANG MIN. No, the appropriation comes from his going to China in the first place.

> *Beat.*

CURATOR. Oh so it's because he's an artist? So are you saying that if he had gone as a *journalist*, then / he…

WANG MIN. No, no, that is not what I am saying. It is not a matter of "should he" or "shouldn't he." What I am saying is that even if he goes as a journalist, he will still be appropriating the stories of others.

CURATOR. But journalism—the ideal of journalism is to collect facts and only facts, right? That's the ideal anyway. But you're saying…

> *Pause. Wang Min hangs her head, massages her temples as though she has a headache.*

Are you okay? Do you have a headache?

WANG MIN. No it's just—there are so many problems with what you just said I don't know where to begin.

CURATOR. Oh.

> *Wang continues massaging her temples.*

WANG MIN. I believe I must simply…understand the…*paradigm* through which I need to speak.

CURATOR. Oh… O—kay…

> *Beat.*

WANG MIN. Let me try this. A newspaper is a highly…curated artifact. You would agree, yes?

CURATOR. Yes.

WANG MIN. When you read the *New York Times* International section, what is your perception of the world?

CURATOR. A lot of problems.

WANG MIN. Death, death. Chaos, destruction. The sense you get from an American "international" newspaper is that the United States is a complex, multifaceted epicenter, and the rest of the world is this…ninth circle of hell.

CURATOR. Well but it's an American newspaper first and foremost, right?

WANG MIN. There is a phenomenon in China where new mothers, desperate for baby boys, *poison* newborn baby girls with mercury found in thermometers. It is said that the Chinese government knows abut this practice but looks away. I was almost one of those so called "thermometer girl" victims. My mother attempted to poison me, but I was saved by doctors in time.

CURATOR. Oh my god! That's—

WANG MIN. You believed that?

CURATOR. I—wait what??

WANG MIN. In one sentence I am able to alter your view of an entire country. I am Chinese so this so-called fact is not questioned. It adds a nice padding to your preconceptions and that is that. What if this James Frey never was caught? Would his writing go down as fact? What if it is discovered Mark Twain embellished parts of his autobiography? Would he be any less revered? And is Ira Glass not a purveyor of stories too? Stories crafted by a thousand subjective choices?

CURATOR. Okay I think I get what you're saying.

WANG MIN. But I want to make *sure* you do.

CURATOR. Well I, I think I do.

WANG MIN. But the *scope* of what I am saying.

CURATOR. Well are you saying that we have a very…hazy relationship to the truth, and within this…kind of foggy haze, Mike Daisey, for example, is not really an isolated case?

WANG MIN. *(Hangs head in quiet despair.)* No. This is not what I am saying at all.

   Awkward pause.

CURATOR. Okay so maybe not an "isolated case." Maybe it's more… his case is relative.

WANG MIN. No. This is also incorrect. This is simply not what I am saying at all.

   Awkward pause.

CURATOR. Okay so what are you saying?

WANG MIN. It is not a matter of isolated or relative "cases." I am saying there are no "cases" at all.

CURATOR. Okay but I think essentially we're saying the same thing, that you can't *blame* Daisey for lying within a lying paradigm, right?

WANG MIN. *(Excited.)* Ah okay, okay!

> *Curator smiles.*

So this is *absolutely* not what I am / saying, but—…

CURATOR. Oh.

WANG MIN. But I think I can explain it this way. *"Blame."* This is an American, Fox News word: who takes whose side, who is to blame. *This* is the noise, the game I am attempting to break apart with this work.

CURATOR. I'm sorry I wasn't trying to make you play a game.

WANG MIN. But you are attempting to understand what I am saying within the context of your own way of understanding things.

CURATOR. How else am I supposed to understand anything??!!

WANG MIN. "Supposed" to "understand"? But nothing says you are "supposed" to "understand" anything!

CURATOR. I'm sorry it just sounds like you're saying—… It sounds like you're saying no one should try and understand or engage or share stories from any other culture because by the very virtue of their differences they can never truly understand the other culture. Is that…anywhere near your point of view?

> *Beat.*

WANG MIN. No, / no not one bit, no.

CURATOR. No, no of course not. Okay so we can't engage? What if we need to *help* another country, if something must be done?

WANG MIN. But why "must" anything be "done"?

CURATOR. Because sometimes there is need, and we are in a position to help, like it or not.

WANG MIN. It is not a matter of "like" or "position." This is still a Fox News, capitalist paradigm.

CURATOR. Sorry I'm not even sure what we're talking about anymore! Capitalism?

WANG MIN. It is not a matter of "talking about" anything. It is a matter of intention. What is Daisey's intention? Altruism, yes. Broadening our perspective on our iPhones, yes. But also, it is for himself. He is a storyteller by trade so he needs new stories to sustain himself.

CURATOR. Okay but what I'm asking is why *can't* you help yourself and help others at the same time?

WANG MIN. It is not a matter of "can" or "can't". It is a matter of: How is a story shaped given non-altruistic strains running through the intention of telling it?

CURATOR. But of course we have our own self-interest in mind. It's impossible not to do that, right? I mean…

WANG MIN. It is not a matter of "of course" or "impossible." This is still the language of capitalism assumptions. We *assume* we must operate from a goal of mutual benefit; *assume* the highest ideal is benefiting yourself and others in tandem. But is this not in essence a paradigm of self-benefit?

CURATOR. So how do you suggest we engage with other cultures? With the rest of the world?

A subtle soundscape enters that will slowly rise in prominence.

WANG MIN. It is not a matter of "engage" or "not engage." It is a matter of intentional awareness. People immerse themselves in other cultures because they are searching for something within themselves, taking parts of the culture that fills a need then leaving the rest behind. It is tasting a peach to better understand an apple; eating bacon and claiming to know the lives of swine.

CURATOR. So we're not allowed to explore cultures other than our own?

WANG MIN. It is not a matter of "allowance" and it is not a matter of "explore." What does explore really mean?

CURATOR. Learn about.

WANG MIN. But learn about to what end?

CURATOR. To know more about this world we all share!

WANG MIN. Please. Do not get frustrated.

CURATOR. But I feel like you're trying to lose me on purpose!

WANG MIN. But we must get lost in order to truly learn.

CURATOR. But you're not coming to my level!

WANG MIN. And yet this evening is structured on *your* terms.

CURATOR. What are you talking about? We worked together on *your piece*! I thought we were on the same page!

WANG MIN. And yet did you invite me here to share my art with the world, or are you playing a game of status by securing a world-famous Chinese artist, a colleague of Yu Rong?

CURATOR. Okay, that's it, I think we're done here.

WANG MIN. Do not give up on me. Stay with me.

CURATOR. I don't want to. You're attacking me.

WANG MIN. I do not mean to attack you.

CURATOR. I don't have to take this.

WANG MIN. Take what?

CURATOR. I don't have to sit here while you question my motivations. You're just a cruel person and that's all there is to it.

WANG MIN. You are within Fox News again. I do not perceive this as cruel.

CURATOR. You *are* cruel! You're humiliating me!

WANG MIN. Humiliation is a construction.

CURATOR. Stop it!

WANG MIN. Cruel is a construction!

CURATOR. Stop it, stop it!

WANG MIN. We cannot stop now. You are letting go of ego.

CURATOR. I don't want to let go of ego. I want to leave.

WANG MIN. You cannot leave. This is good for you. For us.

CURATOR. I feel cold.

WANG MIN. You are having tremors. You are moving out of your comfort zone.

CURATOR. I feel sick.

WANG MIN. This is the path to truth. True truth is never easy.

CURATOR. I need a bag.

WANG MIN. Here.

Wang Min produces a bag. Curator vomits into it.

CURATOR. I don't trust you anymore. This is an abusive relationship.

WANG MIN. It is only abusive because it is founded on false intentions.

CURATOR. I'm not a dishonest person. I'm not a liar just because you say I am.

WANG MIN. A lie is not a bad thing. It is a natural occurrence and is totally understandable. Why do we lie? Because a lie is a new home. A place of return after long and lonely journeys in the dark. Now comes the point in the work where we recognize the interview has changed into something else. Something new. We're unmoored now. Adrift at sea. We are witnessing the birth of a new lie as we speak. We see how in our search for truth we move into something artificial once again. How do we escape lies? A lie is a garden that grows sideways until its sidewaysness becomes straight. It is a feast made from mislabeled ingredients that tastes incredible. It is a documentary. A dollar bill. It is thinking outside the box but then being inside the outside of the box so going further going outside the inside of the outside of the box by going back inside the box to be outside the outside of the box then leaving the box to find another box whose outside has an outer outside outside outside the outside.

Curator starts to cry.

My friend, what is wrong?

CURATOR. I am so lost. Where are you taking me?

WANG MIN. I do not know. It is not a matter of end goals, meaning, landings. It is only a matter of journey.

CURATOR. To where? What can I hold on to?

WANG MIN. Nothing. And that is the point. We cannot stop questioning any truth that is put before us. We negate and keep negating. To stop this thread from unwinding is to rest inside a lie.

CURATOR. But to what end. To what end?

WANG MIN. We will know when we get there. But by the time this happens, it will not be a matter of "get there" anymore.

Music swells. Fade to black.

4.

Suddenly, a new landscape that has elements of either a living room or a green room. It is a comfortable and natural space that the actors lounge in after the show. There may even be a voyeuristic feel to the setup. There may be different concepts to this new environment, ranging from realistic (such as using an actual part of the theater we are in), to the surreal (living-room elements of sofa and table in the middle of a desert). The important thing is that the acting is as easy-going and naturalistic as possible, even as the dialogue turns surreal. Wang Min and Lin Bo are in loungy, everyday clothes. They both have American accents. They are eating fast food and looking on their iPhones. This goes on for a bit. Then…

WANG MIN. Pass the hot sauce?

He does. They eat in silence. They are on their devices. Wang Min watches a video on her iPhone.

Heh… Look at this.

She goes over to him with her iPhone. [Insert improvisation based on specific YouTube video that is viral at the moment.] They exchange a few comments as they're watching. We can hear sounds from the video. They both laugh, Wang Min louder than Lin Bo. After a bit of this, Lin Bo hands it back.

LIN BO. That was great.

He goes back to his device. Mood darkens a bit. A silence.

WANG MIN. How do you think the piece went tonight?

LIN BO. Good.

WANG MIN. Yeah me too.

LIN BO. Receptive audience.

WANG MIN. *(Keeping it light.)* You say that like it's a bad thing.

LIN BO. The real test would be a *Chinese* audience.

WANG MIN. Huh.

LIN BO. Or. Moot point anyway.

WANG MIN. Yeah.

>   *Beat.*

LIN BO. Still not sure about the accent. In the second part.

WANG MIN. When to…

LIN BO. Yeah when to drop it. Or *start* dropping it.

WANG MIN. Yeah. Well it doesn't really matter right?

LIN BO. Right cuz it's…

WANG MIN. All a lie / anyway…

LIN BO. Right, it's a lie.

>   *Pause. They continue eating in silence.*

WANG MIN. Are you okay?

LIN BO. Yeah.

WANG MIN. Positive?

LIN BO. I'm a little down.

WANG MIN. Yeah?

LIN BO. Yeah. But I don't really wanna talk about it.

WANG MIN. Okay. Just let me know…

LIN BO. Thanks.

>   *They eat more.*

I've been thinking about Yu Rong.

>   *Wang Min nods in understanding.*

WANG MIN. What about him?

LIN BO. Were you there when he was ranting about getting cucumbers in his Big Mac? In Beijing…

WANG MIN. *(Laughing, remembering.)* Oh yeah! They had replaced pickles with fresh cucumbers.

LIN BO. Right.

WANG MIN. The Chinese approximation of Western food. Something's always juuust a / little off.

LIN BO. Nooot quite right yeah. Yeah and he had that chant: *(Chanting.)* "Hey ho! Send it back! / No cucumbers in Big Macs!"

WANG MIN. *(Remembering, joining.)* "No cucumbers in Big Macs!"

> *They laugh.*

Of course he wasn't upset about McDonald's in / China…

LIN BO. He didn't want second-/*class* McDonald's.

WANG MIN. Right. A noble cause.

> *They smile fondly.*

LIN BO. I miss him. This *(Motioning to the food.)* just reminded me of him.

WANG MIN. Ah I see. Yeah, American junk food was his weakness.

> *Pause.*

LIN BO. I don't know…would you call it a weakness?

WANG MIN. You think it's good for you?

LIN BO. Or I guess I mean, do you think *he* would have called it a weakness.

WANG MIN. *(Smiling fondly.)* McDonald's? What else would it be?

> *Lin Bo shrugs.*

LIN BO. Maybe…it's not…anything!… Maybe he just…followed the beat of his own drum.

WANG MIN. Right. Which is why he'd consider it *weak* to be *enslaved* by an American corporation.

> *Pause. Lin Bo considers. Slight moment of confusion.*

LIN BO. But see, I think that's what I was getting at. I think I don't see this…blanket Western antagonism you see in him.

> *Wang Min is taken aback for a second.*

WANG MIN. Seriously?

LIN BO. Yeah, I mean he was against consumerism, but I wouldn't say Western influence was his, his cause.

WANG MIN. Who said it was his cause?

> *Pause.*

LIN BO. Maybe what I'm getting at is…okay, so…so the pact was that every project we do will honor his legacy, in some way, and so…

WANG MIN. Wait, you're saying this piece doesn't *honor* him in some way?

LIN BO. No I don't / mean it—

WANG MIN. Because that's a strong statement. He died in prison. And / our whole *mission* is to…

LIN BO. Okay okay. I'm not saying it doesn't *honor* him. I'm just saying…it might not necessarily…reflect…his point of view. That's all.

WANG MIN. Why wouldn't it?

LIN BO. Well it's this…strain of militancy against America, against the West. That's all I'm responding to.

WANG MIN. Well sure, that's *part* of it, but…

LIN BO. Well it's a pretty major part. American hypocrisy, appropriation. Two white *New Yorker* journalists beating up on a Chinese guy, I mean…

WANG MIN. You're…oversimplifying it.

LIN BO. Okay. Fair enough. It was just an impression I had. That's all. It's a great piece. It was just…the connection to Yu Rong I had questions about.

> *Pause.*

Do you hate me?

WANG MIN. *(Smiles.)* No of course not. You're free to feel what you feel.

> *Beat.*

It's just…you didn't think Yu Rong's *A Constitution* was a piece that was critical of America?

LIN BO. No, not at all, actually.

WANG MIN. You didn't think the point of translating the American constitution into Chinese and displaying it next to Mao's *Red Book* was that the American Constitution was on the same level of meaningless propaganda?

LIN BO. No, the point of the piece was that *Mao's* ideals were arbitrary and meaningless and they could have been *Western* ideals for all Mao cared. The point was that *The Little Red Book* was meaningless propaganda.

WANG MIN. Wow. We have…very different opinions about Yu

Rong's work.

LIN BO. He was mainly interested in China.

WANG MIN. Yeah well from my perspective he was mainly interested in Western *perception* of China.

LIN BO. Yeah, wow that's *(Laughs briefly in disbelief.)* very different.

   Long pause.

WANG MIN. You know Yu Rong and I…talked a long time about the piece, *A Constitution.* That's primarily where I was getting this from.

LIN BO. I actually talked a lot about *A Constitution* with him too, that's how I got my interpretation.

WANG MIN. Really.

LIN BO. Yeah.

WANG MIN. *(Smiling.)* But don't you think his…partner…might have, maybe the…deeper insight?

LIN BO. Well in theory, but—… Heh. That's—…

   Beat.

WANG MIN. What.

LIN BO. No that's just great you see him as your partner. I think that's appropriate.

WANG MIN. Appropriate? I mean of course / it's—…

LIN BO. No I mean you shared the same art studio but I never thought—but what I'm saying is I like that. To consider yourselves full-out artistic partners. It's great.

WANG MIN. You're…joking…right?

LIN BO. About what?

WANG MIN. I'm sorry I just don't want to joke around about this, about him, and us. Okay? Is that okay?

LIN BO. Joke…how? I'm not—What are you talking about?

WANG MIN. It's just…sacred to me, you know? What we had. So I just don't want anyone to diminish that, even if it's just joking. I know you didn't have any bad intentions, it's / just…

LIN BO. Wait. Had, as in *had* had? You *had* something?

Beat. Wang looks at him in anger, disbelief.

WANG MIN. Okay seriously, you're actually pissing me off a little right now.

LIN BO. *(Incredulous, a bit angry.)* I seriously—I had no idea! This is news to me!

Pause. Wang glowers at him.

WANG MIN. We were a couple for five years!

Pause. A stare-off.

LIN BO. *(Smiling.)* Okay, okay, I get it.

WANG MIN. *(Smiling in disbelief.)* Get what??

LIN BO. Joke's on me, you caught me.

WANG MIN. What's going on here? Are you okay?

LIN BO. Just stop it, let's just move on.

WANG MIN. Move on from what?

LIN BO. From this joke?

WANG MIN. What joke?

LIN BO. The joke that you and Yu Rong were a couple for five years!

WANG MIN. We were a couple for five years, did you have a stroke or something?

Wang Min stares at him, then starts to laugh. Lin Bo starts to laugh too in relief.

LIN BO. *(Through laughter.)* Okay good. Thank you.

WANG MIN. *(Through laughter.)* For what?

LIN BO. *(Through laughter.)* For stopping this game.

WANG MIN. *(Through laughter.)* No I'm laughing because you're really good.

LIN BO. *(Through laughter.)* At what?

WANG MIN. *(Through laughter.)* At this game you're playing. *(Derisively.)* Yu Rong and I never a couple.

A slight beat. They stare at each other. Then Lin Bo starts to laugh again. Wang Min follows. It is more manic than before.

(Through laughter.) Okay! Good!

LIN BO. *(Through laughter.)* Okay!!

WANG MIN. *(Through laughter.)* You really had me!

LIN BO. *(Through laughter.)* No *you* really had *me!*

    They are both caught in a violent fit of laughter.

(Through laughter.) Yu Rong would have approved. We would have sung praises to your commitment to craft while we made love.

WANG MIN. *(Through laughter.)* You and Yu Rong making love! That's great!

LIN BO. *(Through laughter.)* Yes that's what couples do!

WANG MIN. *(Through laughter.)* And I would know because Yu Rong and I were a couple for five years!

LIN BO. *(Through laughter.)* I think I would have known if that were true!

WANG MIN. *(Through laughter.)* How do you figure?!

LIN BO. *(Through laughter.)* Oh because in case you forgot, Yu Rong and *I* were a couple for five years, and we lived together throughout that time!

    They both laugh hysterically.

WANG MIN. *(Through laughter.)* You guys were just roommates!

LIN BO. *(Through laughter.)* No we were a serious, committed couple!

WANG MIN. *(Through laughter.)* That's what *we* were, until the day he / died!

LIN BO. *(Through laughter.)* Yeah until the day he died!

    They continue laughing for a bit then wind down, exhausted, wiping away tears. The laughter goes away entirely. The atmosphere turns grim.

    They sit in a very long, very uncomfortable silence.

WANG MIN. Speaking…hypothetically…

LIN BO. Yeah?…

WANG MIN. If…if both of us…if both of us…individually, genuinely wasn't playing a game, if we each genuinely thought we were Yu Rong's exclusive significant other for the same five years…then that would mean…

LIN BO. It would mean he had a very elaborate double life.

WANG MIN. Yeah.

> *Pause.*

LIN BO. He'd spend nights, weeks away from home. He could have been with you! Hypothetically.

WANG MIN. He never wanted to show any kind of public affection. It was a rule / of his.

LIN BO. Yep that rule of his.

> *Beat.*

WANG MIN. Five years. We would have been in a haze, if it were true. We all hung out together, we worked together! How would it have been possible!

LIN BO. If anyone could pull it off, it was him.

WANG MIN. He was good.

LIN BO. He was good.

> *Pause.*

Did he say anything about me?

WANG MIN. What do you mean?

LIN BO. Well in your…intimacy…as friends, or *otherwise*, he must have divulged things.

WANG MIN. Why, did he talk about me? To you?

LIN BO. I asked you first.

WANG MIN. I asked you second.

> *Beat.*

So what did he—in your *pillow talk, hypothetically*—what did he think about my work?

LIN BO. Oh, um. I mean / of course he—

WANG MIN. Because he always told me he loved my work.

LIN BO. Well that's great! Yeah, I mean of course he loved your work.

> *Beat.*

WANG MIN. So, to be…perfectly honest. Just for total…disclosure, there were…some aspects to your work he didn't quite…well… connect with maybe?

LIN BO. What do you mean?

WANG MIN. I think it's more… Because he had seen a lot, right? So he was always, always seeing things in other people's work he'd seen before.

> *Beat.*

LIN BO. So you're saying he thought I was derivative?

WANG MIN. Well—… I mean no, the answer's no. But…like for example when you used the image of the smiling man… Because one of his idols was Yue Minjun, who *also* used smiling Chinese men, so…

> *Lin nods thoughtfully.*

But not derivative, that's too harsh.

> *Lin continues to nod.*

LIN BO. I think he thought—and just because you asked—I think he thought your work…might have been a little unfocused.

WANG MIN. Okay don't take what I said personally, I mean / I was just being honest.

LIN BO. I'm not, I'm not, that's genuinely what he said.

WANG MIN. That's what he said.

LIN BO. Yes.

WANG MIN. That my work was unfocused.

LIN BO. Yes.

WANG MIN. What did he say / exactly.

LIN BO. "Wang Min's work is unfocused."

> *Pause.*

No I think it's good we're being honest. And truthful.

WANG MIN. Okay you know what I think?

LIN BO. What.

WANG MIN. I think he was tricking you.

LIN BO. Tricking me? How?

WANG MIN. If he disparaged me—which you're saying he did— then I'm pretty sure it was just a ploy to gain intimacy.

LIN BO. How would lying about what he thought about you increase our intimacy?

WANG MIN. Oh come on that's the best kind of secret—your true opinions of people. Or in this case *supposed* true opinions of people.

LIN BO. How do you know those weren't his true opinions of you?

WANG MIN. There are some truths I know. This is one of them.

LIN BO. Well that's what I think happened on my end—he really liked my work and was lying about it to get closer to you.

WANG MIN. He wouldn't lie to get close to me, he wouldn't have to.

LIN BO. He wouldn't lie to get close to me either.

WANG MIN. Well he's gotta be lying to someone.

LIN BO. Unless he didn't really like either of our work.

WANG MIN. So he's just a big liar? So we never really knew him?? The person we devoted our entire lives to?

> *They sit in a long, charged silence. It is evident each person is going through an internal, silent struggle.*
>
> *Lin Bo rises from his seat. We see him react physically. A suggested sequence: He shakes his head in incredulous disbelief. He pauses. He crouches. He begins breathing deeply, then faster, as if he may hyperventilate. He rises. He paces back and forth like a caged animal, as if wanting to escape the stage. He may make violent movements with his arms. He may swear or mutter violently under his breath. He stops when he's let off enough steam. A beat. He crouches again, back turned away from Wang Min, in a defensive position.*
>
> *The long charged silence continues, until...*

Hey.

LIN BO. Yeah?

WANG MIN. Do you have that...passage he wrote?

LIN BO. Which one?

WANG MIN. About the village? That he sent from prison...the day before he...

> *Lin Bo looks at her. Then decides to oblige. He looks through his iPhone, finds it, hands iPhone to her.*

Wait. Read it. Out loud.

Lin Bo resists.

Please.

LIN BO. *(Reading.)* I was born in a village of no lies.

Slight beat. They look at each other. He goes back to reading.

In this village, nothing was anything but the thing that it was. Nothing was symbol, nor mirror nor pattern. My village had no music, signals, triggers, no house had padding or atmosphere. No latticework of mood, nor righteous hope nor regret. In my life, I have searched for a return to my home village. I have looked for truth but have only seen lies. Within others, within myself. So I began negating all I saw. I negated so much I've negated my own negations. In my life I have searched for truth. To what end? I negated this question too. Because if we are alive there is no end. There is only waiting. Waiting to return to that village of no lies.

Pause.

WANG MIN. I feel…cold.

LIN BO. Me too.

Pause.

WANG MIN. Hey.

LIN BO. Yeah?

WANG MIN. I love working with you.

LIN BO. I love working with you too.

WANG MIN. That's the truth.

LIN BO. It's my truth too.

Long pause.

5.

House lights up. Wang Min and Lin Bo address the audience directly.

WANG MIN. So this piece was inspired by a colleague of ours, the legendary dissident artist Yu Rong, who died in a Chinese prison five years ago.

LIN BO. Before he died he started a new art project that consisted of smuggling words, phrases, and sentences out of prison. They were instructions for works of art that could either be or not be completed.

WANG MIN. We decided to realize as many of his instructions as possible. So that's what we've been doing, and this piece is part of that series. The instructions for this piece were as follows: "Cast doubt upon me. Negate me." That was his prompt.

LIN BO. We chose Mike Daisey as a starting point because of his connection to China and because of his "casting doubt" upon things. But also because Yu Rong had a big soft spot for theater, so we really took this as an opportunity to celebrate that.

WANG MIN. And we were really excited to be able to collaborate with [Insert name of producing company] for this presentation, and for the phenomenal theater artists we recruited: Christopher Chen, [Insert name of director], the design team, and the actors—including myself, I'm a recruited actor too, I'm not really the actual artist I'm pretending to be right now. So thank you to all the theater artists involved, including myself.

LIN BO. We've also had some very generous funders, specifically one corporate sponsor from Silicon Valley, Cupertino. But that's all I'm allowed to say. So that's what's behind this.

WANG MIN. But most of all, thank *you (Indicating audience.)* from the bottom of our hearts, and we'll see you next time.

End of Play

PROPERTY LIST
(Use this space to create props lists for your production)

SOUND EFFECTS

(Use this space to create sound effects lists for your production)